Foreword

I can't have been much more than ten when I stumbled on the wonderful *Complete Limerick Book* compiled by Langford Reed. I was instantly bitten by the bug and have been composing these nonsense rhymes ever since.

I'm not alone in my admiration of this verse form, or of Reed's part in bringing it to public attention. With more enthusiasm than attention to scansion, George Bernard Shaw, no less, wrote

> Langford Reed saved the limerick verse,
> From being taken away in a hearse.
> He made it so clean
> Now it's fit for a queen,
> Re-established for better or worse.

You will find this book slimmer than Reed's, but then he had the whole wide world of limericists to call on, I have only my own efforts. I hope you enjoy them.

ONE:
LIMERICKS FOR ALL OCCASIONS

Cried an out of work actress: 'Disaster!
I've broken my leg: it's in plaster.'
Said her agent: 'Too bad.
Still, she ought to be glad
That someone has finally "cast" her.'

<>

A novice while skiing off-piste
Once muddled his west and his east.
He flew off the edge
Of a rather high ledge
And returned with his skis somewhat creased.

<>

A pious young lady of Trinity
Was taking a degree in divinity.
But she went on the town
With a fellow named Brown
And unfortunately lost her lecture notes.

<>

We all stood in line for a flu jab
And the nurse said: 'We're trialling a new jab.
It may work, it may not –
We don't know what we've got
But we're hoping like hell it's the true jab.'

THE LITTLE BOOK OF RUDE LIMERICKS

Within these pages you will find comic rhymes of all varieties:

- ➢ from the inoffensive… why did that old lady eat 2kg of porridge?

- ➢ to the mildly naughty… what happened to poor Trev in that house of delight?

- ➢ to the downright rude… (you'll have to read the book to find out!)

Discover how a respectable lady deals with an amorous policeman, how the ladies on the *autoroute* don't give their favours away for free and the right way to eat – and pronounce – your scones.

Also by Patricia Feinberg Stoner

Paw Prints in the Butter
Pelicans Can't Read

At Home in the Pays d'Oc
Tales from the Pays d'Oc
Murder in the Pays d'Oc and other Tales

Patricia Feinberg Stoner

The Little Book of Rude Limericks

With illustrations by
Bob Bond

Published in the UK by Fascom 2017

ISBN: 978-0995746244

Cover design by Verité CM
Worthing, West Sussex BN12 4HJ
United Kingdom

Illustrations by Bob Bond
www.footballershappen.com

Warning

Not all the limericks in this book are rude.
In fact, some of them are downright clean.
I apologise to anyone to whom this may give offence.

Or, if you prefer the verse form:

The limerick verse may be seen
As a form that is rude and obscene,
But if you'll take a look
At my little book
You'll find some that are actually clean.

Cried a ten-year-old...

Cried a ten-year-old, 'I've seen a book
Of wonderful limericks. Look!
They rhyme and they're fun
I think I'll do one.'
And that's all the prompting it took.

This book is dedicated with gratitude and affection to

Langford Reed.

Then a man who was standing in line
Said, 'Covid jab? Well, I've had mine.
If it doesn't infect us
It may well protect us.
And the crowd all around him said 'Fine!'

<>

A delusional chap called Mahoney
Confided one day to a crony:
'I've discovered I'm God.
Don't you think that is odd?'
'Not odd,' said his friend, 'just baloney.'

<>

Said a teenager named Nathan Brown
When a girl that he liked turned him down:
'It's true, I've got lots
Of horrible spots,
But I make up for that further down.'

<>

I love to go down to the sea
With a snack and a thermos of tea.
The gulls come and beg
For a scrap of scotch egg
But I'm keeping the sandwich for me.

<>

I'm sick of the cold and the rain
And the wind and the mud in the lane.
As usual the summer
Has turned out a bummer
And I wish it was winter again.

A classical scholar said why
Should I care where I go when I die?
It's perfectly clear
That what matters is here.
The rest is all 'π' in the sky.

<>

While driving along the A40
In a little red car that was sporty
John remarked to Suzette:
'How about it, my pet?
Let's find a lay-by and get naughty.'

<>

Cried a star to a putative mugger:
'Get off me, you horrible bugger.'
Though quickly arrested
He meekly protested:
'I was only attempting to hug 'er.'

Celebration

Hail to the twelfth day of May
For it's National Limerick Day.
Let the poetical clique
Pour scorn on the 'rick
We who write them cry hip, hip hooray.

Matters culinary

I heard them discussing tajine
So I asked them: 'But what does it mean?
Is it lentils or lamb,
Or raspberry jam?
Or escargots in a terrine?'

They said: 'It's a posh word for stew
And it's ever so easy to do.
Take ras-al hanout
And some chickpeas to boot
And some lamb, if you like, chuck in too'

<>

A baker whose surname was Donne
Was annoyed when his friends called him Bun.
'Don't call me a cake,'
He'd protest, 'I may bake,
But when I have finished, I'm Donne.'

<>

A beautiful day, the sun shone
So I sat down and ordered a scone.
A girl all alone
Was eating a scone.
Which one of us, pray, was right-on?

<>

I sat down to eat my cream tea
When a lady adjacent to me
Spread the jam, then the cream
How I wanted to scream!
Cream first is the way it should be.

Points of the compass

A gluttonous man from the east
Once ate forty figs at a feast.
Though he didn't expect
That his tum would object
The poor chap's now sadly deceased.

<>

A knight-errant who hailed from the north
To his squire said: 'Go thaddle my horth.'
Though he spoke with a lisp,
His orders were crisp,
And the squire said 'Yeth, Mathter, of courth.'

<>

A radical chap from the west
Would go out improperly dressed.
He'd call at the vicar's
Wearing only his knickers
A smile, and a grubby string vest.

<>

A rhymester exclaimed with a curse
'I'm writing geographical verse
But as there's a drouth
Of rhymes for the south
Take this one, for better or worse.'

A radical chap from the west...

Ladies! Ladies!

Said a lady who lived in a flat
'There's no room to swing a small cat.
I'll abandon the mog
And purchase a dog
Or possibly, even, a rat.'

<>

A lady who lived in a tent
Lured a man there with evil intent
Cried he 'I am sure
Your intentions aren't pure!
I'm leaving.' And with that, he went.

<>

A social climber who lived in a manse
Decided throw a grand dance
But her neighbours, invited,
Stood firm and united
And sent their reply: 'Not a chance.'

<>

Said a lady who lived in a shoe,
And made it her restaurant too:
'I simply can't thole
A diet of sole
But uppers are fine in a stew.'

TWO:
AROUND AND ABOUT

Said a flighty young lady of Rustington
'I've done all my chores, got my dusting done.
I'll go out on the pull.'
(Which she did, to the full,
Then returned with a smile, all her lusting done.)

<>

Said a stingy old driver of Rustington
'A light on my dashboard has just blinked on.
My son can take care
Of the costly repair.'
That canny old driver of Rustington.

<>

Cried an angry young lady from Goring
'My boyfriend's incredibly boring:
Uninspiring in bed
And, what's worse,' she said,
'I can't get to sleep for his snoring.'

<>

A young vegan fellow of Leeds
Ate nothing but salads and seeds
Till he noticed his ass
Was covered with grass
Intermixed with a fine crop of weeds

There was a young lady of Lancing
Who thought that the waltz was entrancing.
'I orgasm when I glide,'
She gleefully cried,
'It's truly a case of come dancing!'

<>

An elderly lady of Norwich
Ate a two-kilo packet of porwich.
Was it greed? Not at all:
Her flat was so small
She simply did not have the storwich.

<>

A homely young lady of Brighton
Was afraid that her aspect would frighten
Any possible wooer.
So, just to be sure,
She never made love with the light on.

<>

A greedy young fellow from York
Was exceedingly fond of roast pork.
When he saw the dish come
He'd cry, 'Yummy yum-yum!'
And excitedly flourish his fork.

<>

Pretentious? you cannot mean *moi*?
There are others more precious by far
Though I do, it is true
Call NW2
Not Cricklewood but *Crique-le-Bois*.

A greedy young fellow from York...

Said Karl Marx who was living in Cricklewood*
'A bit of the old slap and tickle would
Cheer me no end
But nothing, my friend,
Like a sight of the hammer and sickle would.'

<>

A clumsy young man from Penzance
Invited a lady to dance
She told him: 'My sweet
You have got two left feet.'
So saying, she spurned his advance.

<>

The comma called Oxford's the pits.
I rank it with herpes and zits.
I'm far from amused
When I see it used.
Quite frankly, it gets on my nerves.

*or thereabouts!

THREE:
BELOVED AUNTIE BEEB

To inform, educate, entertain:
The BBC's role was made plain.
But now it's all cookery
And Love Island fookery
And hunting out antiques for gain.

<>

How I long to be left for a while
With eight favourite discs in a pile.
(No cooking! No chores!
No telephone bores!)
On a warm, uninhabited isle.

<>

When Jeremy C threw a punch,
For want of a proper hot lunch,
The Beeb crossly sacked him
But Amazon tracked him
And promptly acquired the whole bunch.

And now Zon's producing *Grand Tour*
I don't watch *Top Gear* any more.
Clarkson, Hammond and May
I would watch any day,
But this lot's a bit of a bore.

The Archers at three-score-and-more

Oh, no! It can't be - not again!
That theme tune! Those women! Those men!
The Archers is heaven
At just after seven,
So roll on the three score and ten.

<>

The Home Farm brigade are a pain:
All Brian can do is complain.
Would that Jennifer might
Be quiet tonight,
And that Kate would go travelling again.

<>

I remember the Archers of yore
Tom Forrest, old Walter and more.
'Me old pal, me old beauty'
Those tones rich and fruity
That the listeners used to adore.

But all the-old timers have gone
The cast and the actors, as one.
A cold or a cough
Has carried them off
Though Jill seems to go on and on.

FOUR:
THE ANIMAL KINGDOM

I'm exceedingly partial to dogs.
I also like warthogs and frogs.
I'm really quite fond
Of the newts in the pond,
And admit to a liking for mogs.

But spiders and beetles and things
With multiple legs and no wings,
You may say they're harmless
But I find them charmless,
Especially the ones that have stings.

<>

The gull on the roof is a menace
And I hate the wood-pidge on the fenace.
The blackbird I love,
And the odd collared dove,
But I'm damned if I know where the wren is.

<>

Purdey, a dog with no bounds,
Is quite the most avid of hounds
For any food proffered,
And if it's not offered
She'll steal it, and claim it was 'found'.

Michael Flanders encountered a gnu
Not, as you'd expect, in a zoo:
Rustington by the sea
(Where he happened to be)
Can seemingly boast of one, too.

<>

A novice who leapt on a horse
Was soon filled with gloom and remorse.
'What possessed me,' he cried,
'To think I could ride?'
At which the steed threw him, of course.

OUR FRIENDS

ACROSS THE CHANNEL

A burly young fellow named Thierry...

UN: VERS COMIQUES
POUR TOUTES LES OCCASIONS

A dashing old man from Toulouse
Would frequently go on the booze,
Though his mild escapades
Brought a headache - in spades! -
And a tongue-lashing from his *épouse*.

<>

Nicole, who hailed from *La France*
Led a life her *Papa* viewed askance:
Running round in fast cars
And lurking in bars
Hissing 'Hello, *chéri*, care to dance?'

<>

A burly young fellow named Thierry
Went to a fancy-dress ball as a fairy
His date said: '*Mon chou*,
That look isn't you –
In fact, it's decidedly scary.'

<>

A saintly young man from Champagne
Was really a bit of a pain.
But he grew much more frisky
On discovering whisky,
And caviar, sex and cocaine.

If you visit *Les Gorges d'Héric*
Watch out for the guide, Dominique.
You should be aware
He has hands everywhere.
Which causes the ladies to shriek.

<>

A stripper from old Montparnasse
Was tattooed in interesting parts.
To roars of applause
She'd haul down her drawers
To reveal Sacré Coeur on her arse.

<>

A vain demoiselle from Alsace
Was exceedingly proud of her ass.
This pert little rump
Was so firm, round and plump
That she had it tattoo'd with 'First class'

<>

There was a young lady from Brest
Who went out improperly dressed.
She was quickly arrested
By a *flic* who suggested
'Some knickers, *mam'zelle*, and a vest.'

<>

There was an old maid of Verdun
As haughty a miss as they come.
She was so supercilious
You'd think she was bilious -
Or had something stuck up her bum.

You tell me the ghost wasn't there
In the spooky old town of Tonnerre,
But I have seen the spectre,
And you would detect her
If you'd stand for a moment and stare.

<>

In Paris an old country parson
Fell in love with a handsome young *garçon*.
The Maître D. said: '*Mon père*,
I shouldn't go there:
He's got a disease he may pass on.'

<>

There's a bar in the town of Auxerre
That's run by Barthélémy *frères*,
Where they'll serve you with whisky
Until you feel frisky
Then sell you their sister '*Pas chère!*'

A question of pronunciation (1)

There was a young fellow from Quimper
Whose penis could not have been limper
A girl he was screwing
Cried 'What are you doing?
This isn't a bang, it's a whimper.'

Or alternatively…

A frisky young lady from Quimper
Attempted to snog with a camper.
But it came on to rain
Which the twain found a pain
And cast on their ardour a damper.

A question of pronunciation (2)

Two young fellows who went on a spree,
In the town that the French call Paree
Have come home with a germ
Which makes them both squirm
And burns quite a lot when they pee.

or alternatively…

You may try but you'll never embarrass
An insouciant native of Paris.
If caught *in flagrante*
They smile and cry '*Santé!*'
They're impossible, really, to harass.

Gastronomical delights

If you dine at St Aubin La Ferté
And the waitress is pretty and flirty
It's so you'll overlook
The food (badly cooked)
And the fact that the cutlery's dirty.

<>

Said a food critic dining at Tours:
'I'm not coming here any more.
The food's so inedible
I think it's incredible
That they gave it not three stars but four.'

The Patron, who heard him, cried: '*Zut!*
You're a crass, unappreciative brute.
Get out, *tout de suite*
On your own ugly feet,
Or you'll leave on the toe of my boot.'

<>

There's a restaurant in old Pézenas
Named after a chap with an ass.
The tourists all think
It's a good place to drink
But the French are inclined to say 'pass.'

DEUX:
VIVE L'AMOUR
(here come the rude ones…)

In France, what you mustn't be doing
Is mixing your words when you're wooing.
Un baiser is a kiss
(Every schoolchild knows this)
But if you '*baise*' you're not kissing, you're screwing.

<>

Said a timid young fellow from Magalas:
'I know I'm a bit of a drag. Alas,
The girls I adore
Cry "Piss off, you're a bore."
And I've never yet managed to shag a lass.'

<>

A myopic young fellow called Ron
Once picked up a girl in Narbonne.
'She' was really a lad
But his sight was so bad
He never detected the con.

<>

A frisky young fellow from Lille
His girlfriend's *tétons* tried to feel.
She told him: 'Michel,
Snogging's all very well,
But if you go any further I'll squeal.'

There's a fine seaside town called Collioure
Where a maiden extremely demure
Met an ardent young swain
Who'd come down from Spain -
And the rest of this rhyme is impure.

<>

While walking one day in the *Bois*
Marianne and Jean-Paul went too far.
Now she nurses the *bébé*
Saying, ruefully, 'Mébé
I should have retained my *sang froid*.'

<>

Cried a frisky young lady from Sète:
'I am never content just to pet.
The more men provoke me
And fondle and stroke me
The keener to screw 'em I get.'

<>

A randy young fellow from Nantes
Said this: 'Since tell me I can't
Shag my sister or mother,
Or even my brother,
I shall climb into bed with my aunt.'

<>

A lady unclothed was once dragged
From the nude swimming beach at Cap D'Agde
By a guy with a hard-on
Who exclaimed '*Dieu me pardonne!*
I shall not rest until she's been shagged.'

A refined young *mam'zelle* called du Maury
Cried: '*Maman*, I'm frightfully sorry.
I've got a new beau
Who's not quite *comme il faut,*
But I just love the size of his... lorry.'

<>

There once was a Frenchman who said
'My girlfriend is not good in bed.
She won't tease, she won't flirt
She just lies there inert
So I'll *baise* with her *Maman* instead.'

'No you won't, you presumptuous pest,'
Cried her *Maman*: 'My girl's not impressed
With your size or technique
(Though you get points for cheek)
So we'll both find a man with more zest.'

<>

Cried a racy young lady from Dijon
I don't mind if you make eyes at me, John.
If you say '*Voulez-vous*?'
With a shrug and a *moue*
I'll answer demurely '*Mais oui*, John.'

<>

A maiden from Brest was distres't
When some nookie her Pa did suggest.
Cried she: 'Ooh la la!
I couldn't, Papa!
But then again, if you incest...'

Cried a gleeful young man from Lorraine
'I am dating the lovely Charmaine.
She's got style, she's got class
And a very nice ass
And, I'm pleased to say, goes like a train!'

<>

An adventurous lady from Lamalou
Once attempted to shag with a camel, who
Rebuked her: '*Mam'zelle*
If you do that I'll yell
And make the skies ring with the ballyhoo.'

<>

A libidinous lad of Marseille
Once invited a girl out to play.
He lasciviously cupped her
And tumbled and tupped her
Then shook hands and said '*Bonne journée.*'

<>

A frisky young lady from Tours
Was exceptionally fond of *l'amour.*
'*Moi, j'adore 'le snog',*'
She would cry, '*c'est un drogue,*
And I must have my fix *tous les jours.*'

Propositioned, a trendy Madame...

Propositioned, a trendy *Madame*
Said 'non' to a randy *gendarme*.
'It just isn't chic
Having sex with a *flic*'
She explained with a trace of alarm.

<>

A damsel from Montélimar
Attempted to snog her Papa.
But her father, much wiser
Was forced to advise 'er:
'Nicole, that is *comme il faut... pas!*'

<>

A wicked old monk from Narbonne
Once tried to seduce a young *nonne*.
'*Non! Non!*' cried the virgin -
Till she saw it emergin'
Then meekly said 'Thy will be done!'

<>

Michele left her native Ardèche
For Paris, all dewy and fresh.
But she soon lost her purity
To a man from the *Sûreté*
Who taught her the joys of the flesh.

<>

A Frenchman whose name was Jean-Pierre
Went out with a girl for a dare
But his preference was
For fellers, because
'Zey 'ave a much nicer *derrière.*'

A randy young *pédé* from Issoire
Was constantly down at the *pissoir*.
When they cried 'You again!'
He'd shrug and explain:
'*Moi, j'aime baiser matin, midi, soir*' *

*(Il y avait un pédé á Issoire
Qui se trouvait toujours dans le pissoir.
Quand on dit 'Encore toi!'
Il s'explique: 'C'est pour ça:
Moi, j'aime baiser matin, midi, soir.')*

(I like to screw morning, noon and night)

<>

There was a young fellow from Rennes
Who was not the most modest of men.
He boasted: '*Sans blague*,
Whenever I shag
The girl gives me ten out of ten.'

<>

There was a young fellow from Bruges
Who went out wearing lipstick and rouge.
Of 'likes' he got few
On Facebook, it's true
But his postbag on Grindr was huge.

Cried a passionate maiden of Orléans:
'You know that it's you I adore, Léon.
But you're so very discreet
With caresses, my sweet:
I could do with a little bit more, Léon.'

◇

A flighty young lady from Nice
Made eyes at the chief of police.
At first he resisted
But when she persisted
He committed a breach of the peace.

◇

A naive young man from Le Touquet
Paid court to a girl with a bouquet.
But she told him: '*Cheri*
Les fleurs sont jolies,
But I'd very much rather have *nouquet.*'

◇

Said the lecherous *prof* to Michèle:
'If you really desire to do well,
With some extra tuition
(And a bit of coition)
I'll see you get top marks, *ma belle.*'

TROIS: L'AMOUR *AL FRESCO*

A couple from St Pierre La Mer
Embarked on a torrid affair.
The pair, well-endowed,
Attracted a crowd
When doing the deed *en plein air.*

<>

There was a young couple from Rouen
Who had the bravura to screw on
The *place du marché.*
It was Bastille Day
And the crowd stood round jeerin' and booin'

<>

There was a young man called Lafitte
Who shagged a girl out in the street.
This didn't alarm
The local gendarme
But *le maire* cried *'Cessez! Tout de suite!'*

<>

An amorous pair from Bordeaux
Did not have a place for... you know!
So they shagged in the street.-
It was indiscreet -
But the crowd all yelled out 'Way to go!'

QUATRE: THE OLDEST PROFESSION

A pretty *putain*, when in Calais
Was caught having sex in an alley.
The judge said: '*Mam'zelle*
You'll be put in a cell
For daring in Calais to dally.'

<>

If you happen to stop off in Gabian
Beware of the whore - she's a scabby 'un.
And when you are through,
Whatever you do
Don't stop: she's a terribly gabby 'un.

<>

A *putain* from Marseillan Plage
Had a penchant for men who were large.
If she found their size pleasing
She'd screw without ceasing
And sometimes neglected to charge.

<>

On the new Autoroute des Plages
If you meet a girl, curvy and large,
Who says '*Veux-tu, chéri?*'
Don't go thinking it's free:
The transaction is strictly *péage*.

A cheerful young fellow named Trev...

An innocent lad from Cahors
Had saved up his *sous* for a whore.
She shagged him all night
Till he begged for respite
Then implacably shagged him some more.

<>

A cheerful young fellow named Trev
Went off for a romp in Lodève.
But he soon lost his smile
When he caught something vile
In a house of delight called Mon Rêve.

<>

At large in the Place de Pigalle
Liliane was one hell of a gal.
For a fistful of *sous*
She would happily screw
Any Dupont, Dumont or Duval.

CINQ: ANATOMICAL ANOMALIES
(ruder still…)

Cried a skinny young lady from Brest
'Physique-wise I haven't been blessed.
And I'm tired of the fun
People poke at my buns
And the absence of curves on my chest.

'So I'm off to a clinic in Nantes
Recommended to me by *ma tante*,
Where they'll give me new lips
And curvaceous hips
And a silicon *téton* implant.'

<>

There was a young fellow from Bourges
Whose tool was the size of a *courge.*
When his girlfriends cried '*Bien!*'
He'd reply '*Ce n'est rien* -
Just wait till you see it engorge!'

<>

Said an ungallant fellow named Claude
My girlfriend's *derrière* is too broad.'
She riposted: 'Mon chien,
Your *chose* is *un rien*,
And your technique is seriously flawed.'

There was a young man of Dinard
Whose tool wasn't terribly hard
But his tongue was so long
And agile and strong
That it earned him a certain regard.

<>

A well-equipped Monsieur cried '*Merde!*
My girl friend to screw is too scared
For my prick's such a size
She just widens her eyes
And screams '*Sacrebleu!*' when it's bared.'

His lady, when asked, replied '*Zut!*
It's true that his *chose* is a beaut.
But it isn't the size
That brings tears to my eyes:
It's what he does with it, the brute!'

<>

Cried a well-endowed man called Jean Luc
Who made the girls squeal with his *truc*
'I'd rather have treasure
Like this, beyond measure,
Than be a *marquis* or a *duc*.'

And finally…

The limerick book is now done
And I hope you'll agree it was fun.
If the verse made you smile
It's all been worthwhile
So goodbye – and thanks! - everyone.

ABOUT THE AUTHOR

Patricia Feinberg Stoner has in her time been a journalist, copywriter and publicist. When writing for her own amusement her preference is for humour, with a particular fondness for comic verse and, especially, limericks.

Her first book, *Paw Prints in the Butter*, is a collection of verses about cats, and is sold in aid of a West Sussex animal rescue charity.

Her most recent book of verse is *Pelicans Can't Read*.

For four years Patricia and her husband were accidental expatriates in the south of France, after kidnapping a small brown and white dog, and her second book, *At Home in the Pays d'Oc*, is a humorous account of some of their adventures there.

This was followed by *Tales from the Pays d'Oc*, a collection of short stories, re-published in 2022 with an extra story, in a companion volume with the third *Pays d'Oc* book, *Murder in the Pays d'Oc*.

A Londoner born and bred, Patricia now lives happily on the south coast of England with her husband, who is also a writer. She welcomes visitors to her Facebook Page, Paw Prints in the Butter. You can also occasionally find her on Twitter @perdisma.

If you have enjoyed *The Little Book of Rude Limericks*, please could you take the time to leave a review on Amazon, Goodreads or wherever you usually post your reviews. It would be very much appreciated.

AND

If you like this book, you might like the following...

PELICANS CAN'T READ

If you have ever pondered the true identity of Puss in Boots, wondered why grey geese fly south or wanted to know what Santa thinks about Christmas, here is where you will find the answers.

Pelicans Can't Read is a collection of comic verse and limericks on these and other diverse subjects, such as the vagaries of the English language and how to tell dragons apart.

PAW PRINTS IN THE BUTTER
a clowder of comical cats in verse

Are there paw print in the butter
And a nose mark on the pane?
Is there fluff beneath the sofa?
THAT CAT's been here again.

"If you have a cat, know a cat or have ever interacted with a cat, this collection of poems will have you chuckling... As with all good writing, this collection can be returned to and enjoyed and shared again and again." - **Ingénue Magazine**

Printed in Great Britain
by Amazon

34614279R00030